3-Minute READING ASSESSMENTS

Word Recognition, Fluency, & Comprehension

Timothy V. Rasinski and Nancy Padak

Grades 5–8

New York • Toronto • London • Auckland • Sydney
Mexico City • New Delhi • Hong Kong • Buenos Aires

Teaching *Resources*

DEDICATION

We dedicate this book to a better understanding of how children read and to a renewed urgency to tailor instruction to meet children's individual needs in reading.

ACKNOWLEDGMENTS

We offer our deepest thanks to the teachers who helped and inspired us in the development and testing of this program. Most specifically our gratitude is extended to Betsey Shanahan, as well as the wonderful and dedicated teachers from the Canton City Schools (Canton, Ohio) and from Parkview Elementary in Wooster, Ohio.

We would also like to acknowledge Terry Cooper and Joanna Davis-Swing of Scholastic Inc., who have been instrumental in our being able to realize this project, and our editor, Merryl Maleska Wilbur, of Scholastic Inc., who helped us put all the pieces together.

Cover design by James Sarfati and Jason Robinson.
Cover photo by James Levin.
Interior design by Solutions by Design, Inc.

ISBN: 0-439-65090-9

Copyright © 2005 by Timothy V. Rasinski and Nancy Padak.
Published by Scholastic Inc.
All rights reserved.
Printed in the U.S.A.

1 2 3 4 5 6 7 8 9 10   40   10 09 08 07 06 05

Contents

Introduction 5

    Time for Assessment or Time for Instruction? 6

    Advantages of *3-Minute Reading Assessments* 6

    Use *3-Minute Reading Assessments* Throughout the Year 6

    What's Included in *3-Minute Reading Assessments* 7

    A Word About Readability Determination 8

    Directions for Administering *3-Minute Reading Assessments* 8

    Scoring and Interpreting the Assessment 9

        Word Recognition Accuracy (Decoding) 9

        Reading Fluency-Automaticity 10

        Reading Fluency-Expression 11

        Comprehension 12

Administration and Scoring Aids 13

Test Passages 15

    Grade 5 15

        Student Form A 16

        Teacher Form A 17

        Student Form B 18

        Teacher Form B 19

        Student Form C 20

        Teacher Form C 21

        Student Form D 22

        Teacher Form D 23

    Grade 6 25

        Student Form A 26

        Teacher Form A 27

Student Form B..28

Teacher Form B...29

Student Form C...30

Teacher Form C...31

Student Form D...32

Teacher Form D...33

Grade 7...35

Student Form A...36

Teacher Form A...37

Student Form B...38

Teacher Form B...39

Student Form C...40

Teacher Form C...41

Student Form D...42

Teacher Form D...43

Grade 8...45

Student Form A...46

Teacher Form A...47

Student Form B...48

Teacher Form B...49

Student Form C...50

Teacher Form C...51

Student Form D...52

Teacher Form D...53

Charts for Recording Results........................54

Class Record Sheet..................................54

Individual Student Record Sheet.....................55

Instructional Ideas for Word Recognition, Fluency, and Comprehension.......57

References...62

Introduction

Assessment is a critical element of successful instruction. Assessment helps teachers determine if the instruction they provide students has resulted in adequate student progress. It allows teachers to identify students who can benefit from a more accelerated instructional program and those who need more intensive instructional intervention and support. And, if the assessment has sufficient precision, it allows teachers to identify a focus for their instruction. In a sense, assessment provides teachers (and schools and parents) with roadmaps that indicate where their children *are* academically, and where they need to go.

Research has indicated that assessment is critical to successful instruction. An international study of reading achievement, for example, found that regular assessment was a key factor associated with student success in learning to read (Postlethwaite & Ross, 1992).

In recent years, state and federal education mandates have required schools and school districts to more closely monitor student performance across a number of content areas and grade levels. These types of large-scale, typically norm-referenced assessments are most valuable for school administrators and policy makers in determining general trends in achievement and recommending policies and procedures at the national, state, and district levels for improving educational quality. For several reasons, however, these kinds of assessments cannot provide teachers with the information they need to make instructional decisions for individual students. One problem is timing—it frequently takes months for teachers to receive assessment results. In some cases a student has already moved on to the next grade before results are available. In addition, the scores on these tests do not lead naturally to instructional changes. Most often, scores simply tell whether or not a student has achieved "proficiency" rather than providing information about diagnostic needs or instructional direction.

Beyond the large-scale, general assessments that provide snapshots of achievement for a large number of children, a number of other reading assessments that lead to more precise instructional interventions are available. Some are commercial standardized tests such as the group-administered *Stanford Diagnostic Reading Test* and the individually administered *Woodcock Reading Mastery Test.* Others, such as informal reading inventories (IRIs) and running records (Clay, 1993) are more informal in nature and are based on teachers' ability to interpret the reading behaviors that they record. Still others, such as the *Developmental Reading Assessment* (Beaver, 1997) and the *Qualitative Reading Inventory* (Leslie & Caldwell, 2000) are hybrids of commercial standardized tests that include a strong informal, teacher-interpretation component. Most of these assessments provide teachers with an in-depth view of their students as readers—their level of achievement and, to some extent, their various strengths and areas of concern in reading.

If there is one major drawback to these sorts of assessments it is time. These and many of the other formal and informal reading assessments that are available to teachers take a considerable amount of time to prepare, administer, and score. The full-scale administration of an informal reading inventory, for example, can take one to two hours to give to a student and another hour (at least) to score and interpret. Although the data obtained from such an assessment are valid and valuable, the amount of time needed to administer such an assessment to every student in a classroom is prohibitive.

Nevertheless, we are seeing instances in many schools in which teachers are expected to administer an informal reading inventory to every child in their classrooms two, and in some cases three, times per year. In a classroom of 25 children, three administrations of an IRI, even if each required only one hour per child, would take 75 hours—the equivalent of nearly three full weeks of school!

Time for Assessment or Time for Instruction?

As valuable as assessment is for teachers, it is in instruction where the rubber meets the road. Students learn as a result of instruction, not assessment. While assessment most certainly must guide instruction, it is no substitute for it. And in schools and classrooms where inordinate amounts of time are taken for assessment, an equal amount of time is taken *from* instruction. In short, time given to assessment is time taken away from instruction. The irony of the situation is that the very thing that assessment is intended to measure—achievement—is curtailed by the time that must be taken away from instruction in order to do the assessment. The 50 hours that it might take to administer an informal reading inventory to every child in a classroom, for example, could have been used to provide reading instruction that would have made those students better readers!

Advantages of *3-Minute Reading Assessments*

With the above considerations in mind, we developed this set of assessments to provide classroom teachers and specialists with a quick way to obtain valid diagnostic information about students' reading achievement. In fewer than five minutes, you can use this system to measure a child's progress and identify areas of strength and concern that may need special and intensive instruction. You will be able to sample a student's reading and determine his or her level of performance in three critical areas—word recognition (decoding), reading fluency, and comprehension. The information obtained from *3-Minute Reading Assessments: Word Recognition, Fluency, and Comprehension* will enable you to monitor student progress over time across these three dimensions of reading, identify areas of special need for individual children, and communicate to parents and others about student progress in reading.

Use *3-Minute Reading Assessments* Throughout the Year

We recommend that you use *3-Minute Reading Assessments* with an individual student three or four times per year at regular intervals—once at the beginning of the school year, once or twice in the middle of the year, and once at the end of the year. You should be able to assess and score a classroom of 25 students in about two hours. Since we've provided four forms for each grade, you will be able to use a different, but equivalent form for each assessment throughout the year.

By assessing students at regular times during the school year you will be able to measure progress in word recognition, reading fluency, and comprehension over the course of the year. You will be able to identify students who are not responding well to your instructional efforts. This will allow you to plan additional or more targeted instruction for those students who are struggling or who are not demonstrating the kind of progress you hope to see.

What's Included in *3-Minute Reading Assessments*

In addition to the background discussion above, this Introduction provides you with a full set of specific directions for administering these assessments. Immediately following those directions we provide scoring and interpretation guides for each of the three major areas covered by the assessments (note that fluency is assessed in *two* distinct dimensions—fluency-automaticity and fluency-expression). Included are

1. the procedure for calculating **word recognition accuracy**,

2. a chart for measuring **fluency through reading rate**,

3. a scale for figuring **fluency through expression**, and

4. a rubric for determining **comprehension**.

In addition to these fully detailed guides (pages 9–12), you'll also find a condensed version of all four guides on page 13. This page is intended to offer you a handy aid that can be torn out and laminated for use during the administration of each passage. We hope it will give you an easy reference point as you listen to the student's reading.

The passages themselves are divided into four grade-level booklets. Each booklet includes the four equivalent forms (A through D) mentioned above. To vary subject matter and maintain interest, the forms are organized by themes: Form A passages pertain to family outings; Form B passages to foods; Form C passages to extreme weather; and Form D to unique individuals. For each form there is a student page, which includes the passage only and is intended for direct use with the student, and an accompanying teacher page. The teacher page reproduces the passage and gives you additional information, such as overall word count and the word length of each printed line. In addition, at the bottom of each teacher page, a scoring section enables you to jot down the student's scores as you figure them, as well as any additional comments.

We strongly recommend recording the data yielded by the assessments, and to make keeping these records easy, we provide two different recording charts. On page 54, you'll find a class record sheet and on page 55, an individual student record sheet. The former enables you to get an overview of class performance at a glance, while the latter helps you track testing data for all four forms for an individual student. You may wish to use both, or simply choose the one that best fits your needs. These charts allow you to highlight areas where performance is below your expectations as well as areas with no growth over time. You may want to address these areas with additional assessment and instruction and bring them to the attention of parents, school administrators, or other teachers.

In order to help you address targeted areas of concern, we include a brief section of Instructional Ideas for each of the three major areas assessed. Pages 57–61 offer instructional suggestions for teaching word recognition, fluency, and comprehension skills. Of course, these ideas are just a springboard for each topic. Entire books of instruction for each area are available!

A Word About Readability Determination

As described above, four different passages for each grade level are presented in separate grade-level booklets. We have spent considerable time checking the readability of these passages before designating each to be at a specific grade level. In doing so, we applied either all or several of the following formulas: the Flesch Reading Ease Formula; the Flesch-Kincaid Grade Level Formula; the Fry Readability Graph; the Spache Readability Formula; and the Dale-Chall Readability Formula. As well, we tapped our own expertise as professors of literacy and researchers to level the passages.

In the end, readability is often a matter of judgment. It is well known that readability results will vary depending on which formula is used and that each formula has its own limitations and drawbacks. That said, there are currently no better alternatives that offer a more accurate or efficient approach to determining grade level for a particular reading passage. Thus, with all this in mind, we feel confident in stating that these passages are on grade level and are equivalent, within each form, in terms of difficulty.

A few additional notes about grade levels and the way we've set up these assessments: We recommend having students read passages at their assigned school-year grade levels because this will help you determine their level of performance on passages that they are expected to master during that school year. In other words, while one third grader may be reading comfortably at fourth-grade level and another at second-grade level, this assessment enables you to determine how well both students will be able to read the grade-level texts you use for instruction. Students whose grade-level performance is excellent may not need repeated assessment. Those who struggle with the grade-level passage will need additional diagnosis. Retesting these students on grade-level test passages throughout the school year will easily allow you to gauge their growth.

Directions for Administering *3-Minute Reading Assessments*

Administering these assessments is simple and straightforward. You simply ask students to read a grade-level passage to you and ask them to recall what they remember from the passage after they've read it. While students read and recall the passage, you monitor their performance for word recognition, fluency, and comprehension. Specific directions are outlined below:

1. Present the student with a copy of the passage from *3-Minute Reading Assessments* that corresponds to his assigned grade level. Ask the student to read the passage orally to you in the way he might normally read the passage. Tell the student that at the end of the reading you will ask him to tell you what he remembers about the passage.

2. The student reads the passage aloud for 60 seconds. If she stops at an unknown word and does not attempt to pronounce it for 2 seconds, or if she attempts the word but clearly has little chance of reading it correctly, tell her the word and ask her to continue reading. During the oral reading, keep your copy of the passage in front of you. Mark any uncorrected errors that the student makes by drawing a line through the missed word. Errors include words that are mispronounced or that you provide to the student and words that the student omits. If a student initially mispronounces or omits a word, but corrects it, write and circle a *c* above the word to indicate it was corrected (and do not count these corrected words as

errors). At the end of the 60-second period, mark the point the student has reached in her reading of the text.

3. After the student has read for 60 seconds, direct his attention to the beginning of the text and ask him to follow along silently while you read the text aloud. Read the passage to the child in a normal and expressive voice. (We ask that you read the text to the student to remove any difficulties he may have had in word recognition or fluency that could hamper his comprehension of the passage. Listening comprehension is a good measure of the students' reading comprehension [Biemiller, 2003].)

4. At the end of your reading, remove the passage from the student's view and ask her to
tell you what she remembers from the passage. After she has retold the passage, ask her if there is anything else she remembers about what she read. If the student is unable or unwilling to retell anything at all from the passage, you may ask for specific information (for example, "What is the main idea of this story?" or "What was described in this story?").

Note: If the student has made few oral reading errors and has not reached the end of the passage within 60 seconds, you may, as an alternative to reading the passage to the student, ask him to read the balance of the passage silently. At the end of the student's reading, remove the passage from view and ask him to retell what he remembers from the reading. Keep in mind, however, that a source of any difficulty in comprehension may be subtle or undetected problems in word recognition or fluency.

After the student has retold the passage, the assessment is complete.

Scoring and Interpreting the Assessment

Scoring *3-Minute Reading Assessments* is simple and quick. The following procedures should be followed:

Word Recognition Accuracy (Decoding)

Word recognition is determined by calculating the percentage of words read correctly in the 60-second oral reading. Divide the number of words read correctly by the total number of words read (correctly *or* incorrectly). For example, if the student read a total of 94 words in the 60-second reading and made 8 errors, the percentage of words read correctly would be reflected in the following fraction:

$$\frac{86}{94} \text{ (86 divided by 94)} = 91.5\%$$

In other words, the student read 91.5 percent of the words correctly.

Instructional reading level is normally marked by a word recognition accuracy rate of 92–98 percent. Independent reading level is normally marked by an accuracy rate of 99–100 percent.

A normally developing student should begin the school year reading grade-level material at an instructional level and, by the end of the school year, at an independent word recognition level. For example, a third grader's performance on a third-grade passage would be instructional at the beginning of the year but independent by the end of the year. Students who perform at the frustration level at the end of the school year, or who do not demonstrate good progress over the year, should be considered for additional assessment to confirm their decoding difficulty. Such students may benefit from specific instructional intervention in decoding (see pages 57–58).

Reading Fluency-Automaticity

One way reading fluency can be measured is through reading rate. Reading rate provides a measure of the extent to which a reader can automatically decode words, thus leaving cognitive resources free for the more important task of comprehending a passage. To determine rate, simply count the number of words the student has read correctly during the 60-second oral read. Words read correctly include those words that were initially misread but corrected by the student. Then, using the appropriate grade level and time period, compare the student's performance against the reading rates shown below.

A student whose reading rate falls within the appropriate range shown above is performing at grade-level expectations. Students who fall below the range may be considered at-risk in terms of fluency-automaticity. Additional assessment may be appropriate for students who perform poorly at the end of the school year or who do not show improvement over the course of the year. These students may benefit from instruction aimed at improving reading fluency (see pages 58–59). Students whose reading rate is above the range limits may be considered to be performing well in fluency-automaticity. However, an important caveat must be noted: Students who read exceptionally fast without attending to punctuation and other phrase boundaries, and who read without sufficient expression may also be considered at-risk in fluency. The following assessment for fluency-expression should be used with all students to give you the fullest picture of a student's fluency skills.

TARGET READING RATES BY GRADE LEVEL

Grade	Fall wcpm*	Winter wcpm	Spring wcpm
1	0–10	10–50	30–90
2	30–80	50–100	70–130
3	50–110	70–120	80–140
4	70–120	80–130	90–140
5	80–130	90–140	100–150
6	90–140	100–150	110–160
7	100–150	110–160	120–170
8	110–160	120–180	130–180

*wcpm=words correct per minute

Reading Fluency-Expression

Reading fluency is more than just reading fast. It is also the ability to interpret a text with appropriate phrasing and expression. You can measure this dimension of fluency by listening to the student's 60-second oral reading and rating it on the Multidimensional Fluency Scale below. Initially you may need to tape record the student's reading and listen to it in order to provide a rating for each of the four scales. Soon, however, you will be able to score the scales on the spot.

At the beginning of the school year, it is not unusual for students to score in the bottom half of each of the fluency dimensions (i.e., to have a total fluency score of 8 or below). However, by the end of the school year, students should be rated in the top half in each dimension when they are reading grade-level material (i.e., they should be able to achieve a total fluency score of 9 or above). End-of-year ratings in the bottom half for any of the fluency dimensions, or a total fluency score of 8 or less, may indicate a need for additional assessment or instructional intervention (see pages 58–59). The Multidimensional Fluency Scale is also useful for helping students evaluate their own reading and in developing their own understanding of fluency in reading.

MULTIDIMENSIONAL FLUENCY SCALE

Rating	Expression & Volume	Phrasing and Intonation	Smoothness	Pace
Circle one →	1 2 3 4	1 2 3 4	1 2 3 4	1 2 3 4
1	Reads words as if simply to get them out. Little sense of trying to make text sound like natural language. Tends to read in a quiet voice.	Reads in monotone with little sense of phrase boundaries; frequently reads word-by-word.	Makes frequent extended pauses, hesitations, false starts, sound-outs, repetitions, and/or multiple attempts.	Reads slowly and laboriously.
2	Begins to use voice to make text sound like natural language in some areas but not in others. Focus remains largely on pronouncing the words. Still reads in a quiet voice.	Frequently reads in two- and three-word phrases, giving the impression of choppy reading; improper stress and intonation fail to mark ends of sentences and clauses.	Experiences several "rough spots" in text where extended pauses or hesitations are more frequent and disruptive.	Reads moderately slowly or too quickly.
3	Makes text sound like natural language throughout the better part of the passage. Occasionally slips into expressionless reading. Voice volume is generally appropriate throughout the text.	Reads with a mixture of run-ons, mid-sentence pauses for breath, and some choppiness; reasonable stress and intonation.	Occasionally breaks smooth rhythm because of difficulties with specific words and/or structures.	Reads with an uneven mixture of fast and slow pace.
4	Reads with good expression and enthusiasm throughout the text. Varies expression and volume to match his or her interpretation of the passage.	Generally reads with good phrasing, mostly in clause and sentence units.	Generally reads smoothly with some breaks, but resolves word and structure difficulties quickly, usually through self-correction.	Consistently reads at conversational pace; appropriate rate throughout reading.

* This scale is an adaptation of one developed by Zutell & Rasinski, 1991. Kimberly Monfort, a third-grade teacher at Bon View School in Ontario, California developed the format above for the scale.

Total Score: _____

Comprehension

How well students understand what they read is the ultimate hallmark of proficient reading. You can get a good sense of a student's ability to understand a text through the retelling. When you are satisfied that a student has told you as much as he or she can remember from the passage, rate the recall on the Comprehension Rubric (see below). As mentioned in the Directions for Administering section, under some circumstances you may wish to have the student himself or herself read the balance of the passage silently. Use the same comprehension rubric to score the retelling whether you read the passage aloud to the student or whether you allow the student to read the passage silently.

A score of 3 or below suggests inadequate recall and comprehension of the passage. At the beginning of the school year, it is not unusual for a student's recall of a grade-level passage to be rated at level 3 or below. By the end of the school year, student performance should be in the upper half of the scale (levels 4–6). Scores in the lower half of the scale at the end of the year should signal the need for a more in-depth diagnosis and perhaps instructional intervention in comprehension. See pages 60–61 for suggested instructional ideas to use with students who may have comprehension difficulties.

COMPREHENSION RUBRIC

◆ Student has no recall or minimal recall of only a fact or two from the passage. **Rating Score: 1**

◆ Student recalls a number of unrelated facts of varied importance. **Rating Score: 2**

◆ Student recalls the main idea of the passage with a few supporting details. **Rating Score: 3**

◆ Student recalls the main idea along with a fairly robust set of supporting details, although not necessarily organized logically or sequentially as presented in the passage. **Rating Score: 4**

◆ Student recall is a comprehensive summary of the passage, presented in a logical order and/or with a robust set of details, and includes a statement of main idea. **Rating Score: 5**

◆ Student recall is a comprehensive summary of the passage, presented in a logical order and/or with a robust set of details, and includes a statement of main idea. Student also makes reasonable connections beyond the text, such as to his/her own personal life or another text. **Rating Score: 6**

ADMINISTRATION AND SCORING AIDS

Word Recognition Accuracy (Decoding)

Divide the total number of words read correctly by the total number of words read (correct and incorrect). For example, if the student read a total of 94 words in the 60-second reading and made 8 errors, the percentage of words read correctly would be reflected in the following fraction:

$$\frac{86}{94} \text{ (86 divided by 94)} = 91.5\% \text{ of words read correctly}$$

Instructional reading level: 92–98%.
Independent reading level: 99–100%.

Reading Fluency-Automaticity

Count the number of words the student has read correctly during the 60-second oral reading. Words read correctly include those initially misread but corrected by the student. Use this chart to interpret results.

Grade	Fall wcpm*	Winter wcpm	Spring wcpm
1	0–10	10–50	30–90
2	30–80	50–100	70–130
3	50–110	70–120	80–140
4	70–120	80–130	90–140
5	80–130	90–140	100–150
6	90–140	100–150	110–160
7	100–150	110–160	120–170
8	110–160	120–180	130–180

*wcpm=words correct per minute

Comprehension

After the student has completed the 60-second oral reading and after you have read the entire passage to the student, remove the passage from view. Ask for a retelling of what he or she remembers. Next, ask if there is anything else the student can recall from the passage. If he or she is unable or unwilling to retell anything, you may probe for specific information (e.g., "What is the main idea of this story?"). When the student has told you as much as he or she can remember from the passage, rate the recall on the Comprehension Rubric.

- Student has no recall or minimal recall of only a fact or two from the passage. **Rating Score: 1**
- Student recalls a number of unrelated facts of varied importance. **Rating Score: 2**
- Student recalls the main idea of the passage with a few supporting details. **Rating Score: 3**
- Student recalls the main idea along with a fairly robust set of supporting details, although not necessarily organized logically or sequentially as presented in the passage. **Rating Score: 4**
- Student recall is a comprehensive summary of the passage, presented in a logical order and/or with a robust set of details, and includes a statement of main idea. **Rating Score: 5**
- Student recall is a comprehensive summary of the passage, presented in a logical order and/or with a robust set of details, and includes a statement of main idea. Student also makes reasonable connections beyond the text to his/her own personal life, another text, etc. **Rating Score: 6**

Reading Fluency-Expression

Listen to the student's 60-second oral reading. Rate it on the Multidimensional Fluency Scale.

Rating	Expression & Volume	Phrasing and Intonation	Smoothness	Pace
Circle one →	1 2 3 4	1 2 3 4	1 2 3 4	1 2 3 4
1	Reads words as if simply to get them out. Little sense of trying to make text sound like natural language. Tends to read in a quiet voice.	Reads in monotone with little sense of phrase boundaries; frequently reads word-by-word.	Makes frequent extended pauses, hesitations, false starts, sound-outs, repetitions, and/or multiple attempts.	Reads slowly and laboriously.
2	Begins to use voice to make text sound like natural language in some areas but not in others. Focus remains largely on pronouncing the words. Still reads in a quiet voice.	Frequently reads in two- and three-word phrases, giving the impression of choppy reading; improper stress and intonation fail to mark ends of sentences and clauses.	Experiences several "rough spots" in text where extended pauses or hesitations are more frequent and disruptive.	Reads moderately slowly or too quickly.
3	Makes text sound like natural language throughout the better part of the passage. Occasionally slips into expressionless reading. Voice volume is generally appropriate throughout the text.	Reads with a mixture of run-ons, mid-sentence pauses for breath, and some choppiness; reasonable stress and intonation.	Occasionally breaks smooth rhythm because of difficulties with specific words and/or structures.	Reads with an uneven mixture of fast and slow pace.
4	Reads with good expression and enthusiasm throughout the text. Varies expression and volume to match his or her interpretation of the passage.	Generally reads with good phrasing, mostly in clause and sentence units.	Generally reads smoothly with some breaks, but resolves word and structure difficulties quickly, usually through self-correction.	Consistently reads at conversational pace; appropriate rate throughout reading.

* This scale is an adaptation of one developed by Zutell & Rasinski, 1991.
Kimberly Monfort, a third-grade teacher at Bon View School in Ontario, California developed the format above for the scale.

Total Score: _____

Test Passages

GRADE 5 BOOKLET:
Student Passages and Teacher Pages

Last week, my family went to the county fair. My father is a volunteer firefighter, so he was working at the fair. My mom and sister and I went to meet him. I am very glad we did; it was a great night. When we arrived, the fair was very crowded and finding my dad was like finding a needle in a haystack. We finally found him because we heard the fire truck siren blaring and knew he would be there. Showing off the fire truck is my dad's favorite pastime; that truck is his pride and joy.

There was a feeling of excitement at the fair. Everyone was happy and having fun. It reminded me of how I felt on Christmas morning when I was hoping for a new video game player. First, my sister and I went on a Ferris wheel that was over a hundred feet high; we could see the whole town from the top. I was truly nervous when we stopped at the top because our car swayed back and forth like a flag whipping in the wind. Shutting my eyes and pretending I was on the ground helped calm me down, but it felt like forever until we started down again. I was relieved when the ride was over.

After that we each got something to eat. I got bright blue cotton candy—blue like a lollipop, not like the sky. It was so sweet it seemed like I was eating sugar straight from the sugar bowl. My sister got a funnel cake covered in sugar. She got so much powdered sugar on her face that she looked like a mime. I thought it was funny, but she didn't. We rode on several more rides and looked at lots of interesting exhibits before we left. It really was a fantastic night.

Name of student _____ Date of testing _____

Grade 5: Form A

Last week, my family went to the county fair. My father	11
is a volunteer firefighter, so he was working at the fair. My	23
mom and sister and I went to meet him. I am very glad we	37
did; it was a great night. When we arrived, the fair was very	50
crowded and finding my dad was like finding a needle in a	62
haystack. We finally found him because we heard the fire	72
truck siren blaring and knew he would be there. Showing	82
off the fire truck is my dad's favorite pastime; that truck is	94
his pride and joy.	98
There was a feeling of excitement at the fair. Everyone	108
was happy and having fun. It reminded me of how I felt on	121
Christmas morning when I was hoping for a new video	131
game player. First, my sister and I went on a Ferris wheel	143
that was over a hundred feet high; we could see the whole	155
town from the top. I was truly nervous when we stopped at	167
the top because our car swayed back and forth like a flag	179
whipping in the wind. Shutting my eyes and pretending I	189
was on the ground helped calm me down, but it felt like	201
forever until we started down again. I was relieved when	211
the ride was over.	215
After that we each got something to eat. I got bright	226
blue cotton candy—blue like a lollipop, not like the sky. It	238
was so sweet it seemed like I was eating sugar straight from	250
the sugar bowl. My sister got a funnel cake covered in sugar.	262
She got so much powdered sugar on her face that she	273
looked like a mime. I thought it was funny, but she didn't.	285
We rode on several more rides and looked at lots of	296
interesting exhibits before we left. It really was a fantastic	306
night.	307

Word Count – 307

Scoring

Word recognition accuracy:

$$\frac{\text{Words correct}}{\text{Total words read orally}} = \text{_____} = \text{_____} \%$$

Fluency-Automaticity: _____ wcpm

Multidimensional Fluency Scale

Expression and Volume: _____

Phrasing and Intonation: _____

Smoothness: _____

Pace: _____

Total Score: _____

Comprehension: _____

Comments and Observations:

Oranges are my favorite fruit. In fact, oranges are my favorite food. There are lots of reasons that I love oranges. The first reason is their color, that beautiful shade of orange. When you look at the perfect orange, you feel like you are looking at a little sun; it seems to glow. The perfect orange is the orange of a brand-new basketball still in the box. It is the orange of a pumpkin just ripe on the vine. It is the orange of the paint you used to paint your first piece of art work in first grade.

The second reason I love oranges is the feel. When you hold an orange, it is like holding a tennis ball of sunshine. You can feel the warmth rising up your arm from that little delight. The third reason I love oranges is their juice. It spurts with each bite like a mini-volcano erupting in your mouth. It drips down your chin like sap oozing from a maple tree in the fall.

The final reason that I love oranges, and the most important, is the taste. Oh, that taste that makes my mouth water, my tongue tingle, and my stomach flip with excitement! Each section holds its own individual surprise.

Sweet or tangy, soft or firm, it doesn't matter. Oranges are definitely my favorite food.

Name of student _____ Date of testing _____

Grade 5: Form B

Oranges are my favorite fruit. In fact, oranges are my	10
favorite food. There are lots of reasons that I love oranges.	21
The first reason is their color, that beautiful shade of orange.	32
When you look at the perfect orange, you feel like you are	44
looking at a little sun; it seems to glow. The perfect orange	56
is the orange of a brand-new basketball still in the box. It is	69
the orange of a pumpkin just ripe on the vine. It is the	82
orange of the paint you used to paint your first piece of art	95
work in first grade.	99
The second reason I love oranges is the feel. When you	110
hold an orange, it is like holding a tennis ball of sunshine.	122
You can feel the warmth rising up your arm from that little	134
delight. The third reason I love oranges is their juice. It spurts	146
with each bite like a mini-volcano erupting in your mouth. It	157
drips down your chin like sap oozing from a maple tree in	169
the fall.	171
The final reason that I love oranges, and the most	181
important, is the taste. Oh, that taste that makes my mouth	192
water, my tongue tingle, and my stomach flip with	201
excitement! Each section holds its own individual surprise.	209
Sweet or tangy, soft or firm, it doesn't matter. Oranges	219
are definitely my favorite food.	224

Word Count – 224

Scoring

Word recognition accuracy:

$$\frac{\text{Words correct}}{\text{Total words read orally}} = \underline{\hspace{2cm}} = \underline{\hspace{1.5cm}} \%$$

Fluency-Automaticity: _____ wcpm

Multidimensional Fluency Scale

Expression and Volume: _____

Phrasing and Intonation: _____

Smoothness: _____

Pace: _____

Total Score: _____

Comprehension: _____

Comments and Observations:

Lightning crashes, thunder booms, and the earth shakes with the power of the storm. This storm is holding us captive in the lobby of the grocery store. Looking out the huge glass windows, we see an angry sky. It seems to be daring us to come outside and make a mad dash for our car. Through the pelting rain we see our brave little minivan. It is just waiting for us to fill its trunk with the week's food and its seats with our bodies.

Another brilliant flash of lightning illuminates the sky. We prisoners of the storm gasp together and change our minds about risking the run. Babies cry and toddlers whimper. Even I, a brave fifth grader, move closer to my mom, just to keep her safe. My mom is getting restless; she is ready to get home. Her ice cream is melting. The crowd at the front of the store is getting bigger. Every now and then a young man darts out into the weather. We all watch as he gets battered by the rains and struggles to make it into his car. Then we all watch as he drives away, freed from the stuffy store that we are trapped in.

I know that my mom is about to make that courageous run. She puts my sister's hand in mine and tells me not to move. My sister and I watch in amazement as she runs into the rain. She runs like an Olympic athlete and reaches the car in no time at all. We watch as our brave little minivan drives to the door. Grocery bags in hand, my sister and I make our dangerous trip. We have beaten the storm. Mom has saved the day.

Name of student _____ Date of testing _____

Grade 5: Form C

Lightning crashes, thunder booms, and the earth shakes	8
with the power of the storm. This storm is holding us captive	20
in the lobby of the grocery store. Looking out the huge	31
glass windows, we see an angry sky. It seems to be daring	43
us to come outside and make a mad dash for our car.	55
Through the pelting rain we see our brave little minivan. It is	67
just waiting for us to fill its trunk with the week's food and its	81
seats with our bodies.	85
Another brilliant flash of lightning illuminates the sky.	93
We prisoners of the storm gasp together and change our	103
minds about risking the run. Babies cry and toddlers	112
whimper. Even I, a brave fifth grader, move closer to my	123
mom, just to keep her safe. My mom is getting restless; she is	136
ready to get home. Her ice cream is melting. The crowd at	148
the front of the store is getting bigger. Every now and then	160
a young man darts out into the weather. We all watch as	172
he gets battered by the rains and struggles to make it into	184
his car. Then we all watch as he drives away, freed from the	197
stuffy store that we are trapped in.	204
I know that my mom is about to make that courageous	215
run. She puts my sister's hand in mine and tells me not to	228
move. My sister and I watch in amazement as she runs into	240
the rain. She runs like an Olympic athlete and reaches the	251
car in no time at all. We watch as our brave little minivan	264
drives to the door. Grocery bags in hand, my sister and I	276
make our dangerous trip. We have beaten the storm. Mom	286
has saved the day.	290

Word Count – 290

Scoring

Word recognition accuracy:

$$\frac{\text{Words correct}}{\text{Total words read orally}} = \underline{\hspace{1cm}} = \underline{\hspace{1cm}} \%$$

Fluency-Automaticity: _____ wcpm

Multidimensional Fluency Scale

Expression and Volume: _____

Phrasing and Intonation: _____

Smoothness: _____

Pace: _____

Total Score: _____

Comprehension: _____

Comments and Observations:

John has been my friend for as long as I can remember. Our houses are next to each other. In the winter, when the last of the leaves are off the trees, I can see into his family room from my window.

When I first met John, he was as shy as a field mouse. He got nervous every time I came near and seemed terrified of me. Once we got to know each other better, John came out of his shell. We discovered that we liked all the same things and disliked the same things, too. My mom said we should have been born brothers because we're so similar.

John and I play together every day now. Depending on how we feel, we either play at my house or his, or lots of times we venture outside to find something interesting to do. Together John and I make a great team. Someday we will open a detective agency and solve mysteries. For now we just pretend, and it is great fun.

We are no longer in the same class at school, but we still get together every day. Homework is not as much fun since we can't do it together anymore, but John still is my best friend. There is nothing as good as a friend like John.

Name of student _____ Date of testing _____

Grade 5: Form D

John has been my friend for as long as I can remember.	*12*
Our houses are next to each other. In the winter, when the	*24*
last of the leaves are off the trees, I can see into his family	*38*
room from my window.	*42*
When I first met John, he was as shy as a field mouse.	*55*
He got nervous every time I came near and seemed	*65*
terrified of me. Once we got to know each other better,	*76*
John came out of his shell. We discovered that we liked all	*88*
the same things and disliked the same things, too. My mom	*99*
said we should have been born brothers because we're so	*109*
similar.	*110*
John and I play together every day now. Depending on	*120*
how we feel, we either play at my house or his, or lots of	*134*
times we venture outside to find something interesting to	*143*
do. Together John and I make a great team. Someday we	*154*
will open a detective agency and solve mysteries. For now	*164*
we just pretend, and it is great fun.	*172*
We are no longer in the same class at school, but we	*184*
still get together every day. Homework is not as much fun	*195*
since we can't do it together anymore, but John still is my	*207*
best friend. There is nothing as good as a friend like John.	*219*

Word Count – 219

Scoring

Word recognition accuracy:

$$\frac{\text{Words correct}}{\text{Total words read orally}} = \underline{\hspace{2cm}} = \underline{\hspace{2cm}} \%$$

Fluency-Automaticity: _____ wcpm

Multidimensional Fluency Scale

Expression and Volume: _____

Phrasing and Intonation: _____

Smoothness: _____

Pace: _____

Total Score: _____

Comprehension: _____

Comments and Observations:

Test Passages

GRADE 6 BOOKLET:

Student Passages and Teacher Pages

Have you ever been to an amusement park? On Labor Day weekend, my family and I went to the largest one in our state. During our visit we rode many rides and saw some great shows. The best part was the roller coasters. My brother Jason and I had a mission to go on every coaster at least once, and we accomplished it. We even went on several of the coasters twice.

The recently constructed Shredder was the first coaster that we tried. It is the tallest, largest, and most daunting coaster I have ever seen. We didn't have to wait in line too long to experience The Shredder. Once on board, a large metal bar held my body in place, and two pads surrounded either side of my head. It was intimidating to stand there and look up, knowing the ride was about to begin. My heart was beating like drums at a rock concert, and as we slowly climbed up the track, I felt as if someone was turning up the volume of my heartbeat. It got louder and louder by the second. Suddenly, the climb was over, and we began to plunge. It felt as if I were completely free-falling to the ground. I was afraid that the safety bar would release. But to my relief, it didn't.

Upon reaching the bottom, we started to whip around bends and fly upside down as if we were in a balloon that was losing air. My head was knocked back and forth between the pads like a pinball. Up and down we went, round and round, upside down and back again. It seemed like the ride would never stop, and then all of a sudden it was over. My brother and I had a few minutes of rest, and after we regained our composure, we were ready for more.

Name of student _____ Date of testing _____

Grade 6: Form A

Have you ever been to an amusement park? On Labor	10
Day weekend, my family and I went to the largest one in	22
our state. During our visit we rode many rides and saw some	34
great shows. The best part was the roller coasters. My	44
brother Jason and I had a mission to go on every coaster at	57
least once, and we accomplished it. We even went on	67
several of the coasters twice.	72
The recently constructed Shredder was the first coaster	80
that we tried. It is the tallest, largest, and most daunting	91
coaster I have ever seen. We didn't have to wait in line too	104
long to experience The Shredder. Once on board, a large	114
metal bar held my body in place, and two pads	124
surrounded either side of my head. It was intimidating to	134
stand there and look up, knowing the ride was about to	145
begin. My heart was beating like drums at a rock concert,	156
and as we slowly climbed up the track, I felt as if someone	169
was turning up the volume of my heartbeat. It got louder	180
and louder by the second. Suddenly, the climb was over,	190
and we began to plunge. It felt as if I were completely	202
free-falling to the ground. I was afraid that the safety bar	213
would release. But to my relief, it didn't.	221
Upon reaching the bottom, we started to whip around	230
bends and fly upside down as if we were in a balloon that	243
was losing air. My head was knocked back and forth	253
between the pads like a pinball. Up and down we went,	264
round and round, upside down and back again. It seemed	274
like the ride would never stop, and then all of a sudden it	287
was over. My brother and I had a few minutes of rest, and	300
after we regained our composure, we were ready for more.	310

Word Count – 310

Scoring

Word recognition accuracy:

$$\frac{\text{Words correct}}{\text{Total words read orally}} = _____ = _____ \%$$

Fluency-Automaticity: _____ wcpm

Multidimensional Fluency Scale

Expression and Volume: _____

Phrasing and Intonation: _____

Smoothness: _____

Pace: _____

Total Score: _____

Comprehension: _____

Comments and Observations:

Sticky, gooey, creamy, and delicious is how I describe peanut butter. There is nothing else like it on the planet. Smooth or crunchy, on bread or alone, it's the world's greatest food. While dangerous for some with allergies, peanut butter is a food that should not be missed by the rest. Peanut butter is good in a sandwich, on a cracker, on celery, on a pretzel, mixed with chocolate, or just on its own.

Its taste is one that many people love. It reminds adults of lunches as a child, causes teenagers to race home for a snack, and makes babies bang on their high chairs like animals, crying for more. The color of peanut butter is like that of autumn leaves, just as they are losing their last bits of color. It is the color of caramel bubbling on the stove. Each bite of peanut butter bursts with flavor.

Sitting on the pantry shelf it seems to call my name, even when I am not hungry. It tempts me to take one little spoonful, and if I take one, I am sure to take more. Peanut butter is my first thought when I want a snack. It is the first thing I look for in the pantry when I get home from school and the first thing on the grocery list every week.

Name of student _____ Date of testing _____

Grade 6: Form B

Sticky, gooey, creamy, and delicious is how I describe	9
peanut butter. There is nothing else like it on the planet.	20
Smooth or crunchy, on bread or alone, it's the world's	30
greatest food. While dangerous for some with allergies,	38
peanut butter is a food that should not be missed by the	50
rest. Peanut butter is good in a sandwich, on a cracker, on	62
celery, on a pretzel, mixed with chocolate, or just on its own.	74
Its taste is one that many people love. It reminds adults	85
of lunches as a child, causes teenagers to race home for a	97
snack, and makes babies bang on their high chairs like	107
animals crying for more. The color of peanut butter is like	118
that of autumn leaves, just as they are losing their last bits	130
of color. It is the color of caramel bubbling on the stove.	142
Each bite of peanut butter bursts with flavor.	150
Sitting on the pantry shelf it seems to call my name,	161
even when I am not hungry. It tempts me to take one little	174
spoonful, and if I take one, I am sure to take more. Peanut	187
butter is my first thought when I want a snack. It is the first	201
thing I look for in the pantry when I get home from school	214
and the first thing on the grocery list every week.	224

Word Count – 224

Scoring

Word recognition accuracy:

$\dfrac{\text{Words correct}}{\text{Total words read orally}}$ = _____ = _____ %

Fluency-Automaticity: _____ wcpm

Multidimensional Fluency Scale

Expression and Volume: _____

Phrasing and Intonation: _____

Smoothness: _____

Pace: _____

Total Score: _____

Comprehension: _____

Comments and Observations:

The air was crisp and clear after last night's rain; it was one of those fall days that you wait for. Everything was perfect. The leaves that still clung to the trees were a kaleidoscope of colors: red, yellow, orange, brown, and green. Those that had fallen littered the street like remnants of a party that had gone on the night before.

Stepping out of my warm house for my early morning walk was like stepping into a memory of days that had gone before. The cool air met me, and I took a deep breath, drawing in the lovely scents of the season. The crispness of the air is what makes this type of day so special.

Thoughts of backyard football, leaf piles, and warm coats and hats filled my mind as I crunched down the leaf-covered sidewalk. I had a small start of excitement and anticipation as I thought of the warm turkey and gravy that I would eat at next week's Thanksgiving feast. A few birds called to me from the trees. Squirrels darted out of my path as they hunted for those final nuts to keep them fat and full over the upcoming winter. The few cars that did venture down this street drove slowly, aware that wet leaves are a deceptive hazard. The cars seemed to be showing their own form of respect for this special morning. It was the type of fall day you dream of, the type that you remember for the rest of your life.

Name of student _____ Date of testing _____

Grade 6: Form C

The air was crisp and clear after last night's rain; it was	12
one of those fall days that you wait for. Everything was	23
perfect. The leaves that still clung to the trees were a	34
kaleidoscope of colors: red, yellow, orange, brown, and	42
green. Those that had fallen littered the street like remnants	52
of a party that had gone on the night before.	62
Stepping out of my warm house for my early morning	72
walk was like stepping into a memory of days that had	83
gone before. The cool air met me, and I took a deep	95
breath, drawing in the lovely scents of the season. The	105
crispness of the air is what makes this type of day so	117
special.	118
Thoughts of backyard football, leaf piles, and warm	126
coats and hats filled my mind as I crunched down the	137
leaf-covered sidewalk. I had a small start of excitement	146
and anticipation as I thought of the warm turkey and gravy	157
that I would eat at next week's Thanksgiving feast. A few	168
birds called to me from the trees. Squirrels darted out of my	180
path as they hunted for those final nuts to keep them fat	192
and full over the upcoming winter. The few cars that did	203
venture down this street drove slowly, aware that wet	212
leaves are a deceptive hazard. The cars seemed to be	222
showing their own form of respect for this special morning.	232
It was the type of fall day you dream of, the type that you	246
remember for the rest of your life.	253

Word Count – 253

Scoring

Word recognition accuracy:

$$\frac{\text{Words correct}}{\text{Total words read orally}} = \underline{\hspace{2cm}} = \underline{\hspace{2cm}}\%$$

Fluency-Automaticity: _____ wcpm

Multidimensional Fluency Scale

Expression and Volume: _____

Phrasing and Intonation: _____

Smoothness: _____

Pace: _____

Total Score: _____

Comprehension: _____

Comments and Observations:

Ms. Banks, an elderly woman, lives down the street from me. I used to find her quite frightening. Her house sits back in thick woods, which close over it like a cave. The sides of her home are encompassed by ivy, with stems hanging off like locks of hair. The house seems alive, waiting to snare an unsuspecting victim.

When I was younger, my mother made me take Ms. Banks's newspaper to her front door every morning as we walked to the bus stop. My mom explained that Ms. Banks had difficulty walking and that there was no reason my young legs couldn't do some of her walking for her. Each day as I skulked up the dark driveway, I felt that I was approaching a haunted house that held secrets I did not want to know. It was always so silent, as if the birds and insects were afraid of this place, too.

On the street I always walked the other way when Ms. Banks approached. She seemed to creep when she walked—like a turtle making its way across the path. I had never encountered anyone so old.

One morning I was placing her paper on her step when the door opened. There was Ms. Banks armed with a bag of cookies and a flower for my mother. There was no time for us to come in, but she thanked us both for helping her with her paper. After speaking with Ms. Banks, I realized that I had judged her before I knew her. It turned out she was a kind old woman who just needed a little bit of help and a bit of company, too.

Name of student _____ Date of testing _____

Grade 6: Form D

Ms. Banks, an elderly woman, lives down the street from	10
me. I used to find her quite frightening. Her house sits back	22
in thick woods, which close over it like a cave. The sides of	35
her home are encompassed by ivy with stems hanging off	45
like locks of hair. The house seems alive, waiting to snare an	57
unsuspecting victim.	59
When I was younger, my mother made me take Ms.	69
Banks's newspaper to her front door every morning as we	79
walked to the bus stop. My mom explained that Ms. Banks	90
had difficulty walking and that there was no reason my	100
young legs couldn't do some of her walking for her. Each	111
day as I skulked up the dark driveway, I felt that I was	124
approaching a haunted house that held secrets I did not	134
want to know. It was always so silent, as if the birds and	147
insects were afraid of this place, too.	154
On the street I always walked the other way when	164
Ms. Banks approached. She seemed to creep when she	173
walked—like a turtle making its way across the path. I had	185
never encountered anyone so old.	190
One morning I was placing her paper on her step when	201
the door opened. There was Ms. Banks armed with a bag of	213
cookies and a flower for my mother. There was no time for	225
us to come in, but she thanked us both for helping her with	238
her paper. After speaking with Ms. Banks, I realized that I	249
had judged her before I knew her. It turned out she was a	262
kind old woman who just needed a little bit of help and a	275
bit of company, too.	279

Word Count – 279

Scoring

Word recognition accuracy:

$$\frac{\text{Words correct} \rule{3cm}{0.4pt}}{\text{Total words read orally}} = \rule{2cm}{0.4pt} = \rule{1.5cm}{0.4pt} \%$$

Fluency-Automaticity: _____ wcpm

Multidimensional Fluency Scale

Expression and Volume: _____

Phrasing and Intonation: _____

Smoothness: _____

Pace: _____

Total Score: _____

Comprehension: _____

Comments and Observations:

Test Passages

GRADE 7 BOOKLET:

Student Passages and Teacher Pages

Recently, my father took me on a fishing trip in the Atlantic Ocean. We decided that just the two of us would go, and my mom and little sister would remain at home. The drive to get to the coast was extremely long. I had so much anticipation building in me that the drive seemed interminable. I was reminded of waiting for my turn on the playground equipment when I was a little girl.

My father has a passion for fishing, and he was excited to get out on the water again. The instant we arrived at the hotel, he wanted to get to the docks. After carefully comparing prices and sizes, my dad selected a vessel to charter, and we were off. Grayish blue and calm, the waters seemed to be inviting us on an adventure. Our captain was very efficient and got us right to work preparing our equipment. We organized the rods, reels, lines, and bait, and once the captain cut the engines, we cast our lines into the sea.

It was pleasant waiting for our bait to tempt some aquatic creature. My dad regaled me with stories of past fishing trips and the big fish that always seemed to get away. His stories may have been exaggerated, but I enjoyed listening to them. With a few nibbles here and there, the day passed quickly. We may not have caught the whopper, but it was a great day nevertheless. My dad and I have decided to make this an annual trip. I am anxiously awaiting next year already.

Name of student _____ Date of testing _____

Grade 7: Form A

Recently, my father took me on a fishing trip in the Atlantic	12
Ocean. We decided that just the two of us would go, and my	25
mom and little sister would remain at home. The drive to get to the	39
coast was extremely long. I had so much anticipation building in	50
me that the drive seemed interminable. I was reminded of waiting	61
for my turn on the playground equipment when I was a little girl.	74
My father has a passion for fishing, and he was excited to get	87
out on the water again. The instant we arrived at the hotel, he	100
wanted to get to the docks. After carefully comparing prices and	111
sizes, my dad selected a vessel to charter, and we were off.	123
Grayish blue and calm, the waters seemed to be inviting us on an	136
adventure. Our captain was very efficient and got us right to work	148
preparing our equipment. We organized the rods, reels, lines, and	158
bait, and once the captain cut the engines, we cast our lines into	171
the sea.	173
It was pleasant waiting for our bait to tempt some aquatic	184
creature. My dad regaled me with stories of past fishing trips and	196
the big fish that always seemed to get away. His stories may have	209
been exaggerated, but I enjoyed listening to them. With a few	220
nibbles here and there, the day passed quickly. We may not have	232
caught the whopper, but it was a great day nevertheless. My dad	244
and I have decided to make this an annual trip. I am anxiously	257
awaiting next year already.	261

Word Count – 261

Scoring

Word recognition accuracy:

$$\frac{\text{Words correct}}{\text{Total words read orally}} = _____ = _____ \%$$

Fluency-Automaticity: _____ wcpm

Multidimensional Fluency Scale

Expression and Volume: _____

Phrasing and Intonation: _____

Smoothness: _____

Pace: _____

Total Score: _____

Comprehension: _____

Comments and Observations:

I crave spaghetti, a mouth-watering delicacy. The long and tender noodles call to me to be slurped and gobbled. When lying on the plate, these noodles look like a warm, comfortable nest waiting for its family to return to roost. The steaming sauce is a hearty red, reminding me of the fresh, plump tomatoes from which the sauce is created. Noodles and sauce together emit a scent that makes my mouth water; time stops for me and I can think of nothing else but spaghetti.

As the steam from the hot noodles and boiling sauce rises to meet my nostrils, I feel complete happiness. Nothing else could possibly be so fabulous, so fantastic, and so truly delicious as this pasta dish. I linger with the warmth on my face and then attack the plate like a starving toddler with her morning cereal and milk.

The taste is one that I know so well, but never tire of. It is like eating comfort and satisfaction from a spoon and fork. Sauce flicks off in all directions like water spraying from a hose. Streaks of red stain my chin. I have no time for neatness; my spaghetti is getting cold. I take each bite with purpose and determination; this is important work, not to be carried out by just anyone. My initial reaction to the empty plate staring up at me is one of grave disappointment. But then, as my stomach realizes the wonder of what it has just received, a sense of contentment settles in. Yet again, that amazing invention—spaghetti—has proved its worth.

Name of student _____ Date of testing _____

Grade 7: Form B

I crave spaghetti, a mouth-watering delicacy. The long and	9
tender noodles call to me to be slurped and gobbled. When lying	21
on the plate, these noodles look like a warm, comfortable nest	32
waiting for its family to return to roost. The steaming sauce is a	45
hearty red, reminding me of the fresh, plump tomatoes from which	56
the sauce is created. Noodles and sauce together emit a scent	67
that makes my mouth water; time stops for me and I can think of	81
nothing else but spaghetti.	85

As the steam from the hot noodles and boiling sauce rises to 97
meet my nostrils, I feel complete happiness. Nothing else could 107
possibly be so fabulous, so fantastic, and so truly delicious as this 119
pasta dish. I linger with the warmth on my face and then attack 132
the plate like a starving toddler with her morning cereal and milk. 144

The taste is one that I know so well, but never tire of. It is like 160
eating comfort and satisfaction from a spoon and fork. Sauce 170
flicks off in all directions like water spraying from a hose. Streaks of 183
red stain my chin. I have no time for neatness; my spaghetti is 196
getting cold. I take each bite with purpose and determination; this 207
is important work, not to be carried out by just anyone. My initial 220
reaction to the empty plate staring up at me is one of grave 233
disappointment. But then, as my stomach realizes the wonder of 243
what it has just received, a sense of contentment settles in. Yet 255
again, that amazing invention—spaghetti—has proved its worth. 264

Word Count – 264

Scoring

Word recognition accuracy:

Words correct
———————————— = _____ = _____ %
Total words read orally

Fluency-Automaticity: _____ wcpm

Multidimensional Fluency Scale

Expression and Volume: _____

Phrasing and Intonation: _____

Smoothness: _____

Pace: _____

Total Score: _____

Comprehension: _____

Comments and Observations:

The word *freezing* is not sufficient to describe the biting cold that is encompassing my body at this very moment. My bones are frigid, stiff, and sore; my inner being is frozen and dark; my legs are numb; and no warmth at all remains in my body. Were you to take my temperature right now, it would register 32 degrees or below.

The wait for the bus has seemed interminable and intolerable. I stand out here alone, forlorn and solitary, waiting for the yellow and blue vehicle that represents relief and safety. The air around me seems to crackle like ice breaking apart with each breath I inhale. The condensation coming from my mouth is like the vapor from a locomotive. It hangs in the air like a speech bubble from a cartoon character. My thoughts, muddled by the intense cold, somehow arrive at the idea that I need to stomp my feet to help sensation return. As each foot meets the pavement, a wave of pain travels up my leg like lightning. Though it hurts, I am relieved by the pain, as it means my legs still have the capacity to feel!

I twist around to look back at my house, and there, inside the steamy window, is my mom observing me like a proud mother hen watching her chick take her first steps toward independence. She seems surreal as she waves gaily to me; she is dressed only in her warm cozy pajamas and looks completely comfortable. Is it possible that she cannot be experiencing this torturous cold? How can she escape this? I turn away, not wanting her to see how wounded I am by her comfort. Off in the distance I see a glint of yellow and blue. Is it possible? Will I survive this frozen ordeal? Yes, the bus has arrived, and I am saved for another day.

Name of student _____ Date of testing _____

Grade 7: Form C

The word *freezing* is not sufficient to describe the biting cold	11
that is encompassing my body at this very moment. My bones are	23
frigid, stiff, and sore; my inner being is frozen and dark; my legs are	37
numb; and no warmth at all remains in my body. Were you to take	51
my temperature right now, it would register 32 degrees or below.	62
The wait for the bus has seemed interminable and intolerable.	72
I stand out here alone, forlorn and solitary, waiting for the yellow	84
and blue vehicle that represents relief and safety. The air around	95
me seems to crackle like ice breaking apart with each breath I	107
inhale. The condensation coming from my mouth is like the vapor	118
from a locomotive. It hangs in the air like a speech bubble from a	132
cartoon character. My thoughts, muddled by the intense cold,	141
somehow arrive at the idea that I need to stomp my feet to help	155
sensation return. As each foot meets the pavement, a wave of	166
pain travels up my leg like lightning. Though it hurts, I am relieved	179
by the pain, as it means my legs still have the capacity to feel!	193
I twist around to look back at my house, and there, inside the	206
steamy window, is my mom observing me like a proud mother hen	218
watching her chick take her first steps toward independence. She	228
seems surreal as she waves gaily to me; she is dressed only in her	242
warm cozy pajamas and looks completely comfortable. Is it	251
possible that she cannot be experiencing this torturous cold? How	261
can she escape this? I turn away, not wanting her to see how	274
wounded I am by her comfort. Off in the distance I see a glint of	289
yellow and blue. Is it possible? Will I survive this frozen ordeal? Yes,	302
the bus has arrived, and I am saved for another day.	313

Word Count – 313

Scoring

Word recognition accuracy:

$$\frac{\text{Words correct}}{\text{Total words read orally}} = _____ = _____ \%$$

Fluency-Automaticity: _____ wcpm

Multidimensional Fluency Scale

Expression and Volume: _____

Phrasing and Intonation: _____

Smoothness: _____

Pace: _____

Total Score: _____

Comprehension: _____

Comments and Observations:

Mr. Winters is the most unusual teacher I have ever seen. He is not unattractive, yet he certainly wouldn't be defined as handsome. He is extremely tall and pencil-thin. Looking at him, you feel a jolt of surprise; you definitely have to take a second look.

Peculiar is probably the word to describe his looks. A wild shock of mousy brown hair rests on his head like a squirrel's nest abandoned for the winter. His long, pointy face brings to mind images of rocky cliffs, with his nose being the tallest mountain of them all. His glasses, which constantly need to be pushed up, are like a climber desperately trying to scale this peak. Yet, the goal of reaching the zenith consistently slips out of the glasses' grasp. Mr. Winters is always adorned in brown. An occasional glimpse of color may be spotted on a handkerchief that peeks from the pocket of his suit coat.

What makes Mr. Winters truly remarkable is his voice. Listeners expect a high, frail voice to match his frame, and so it is a true shock to hear the deep, gravelly boom that escapes his lips. The combination of weak and strong that he embodies makes him intriguing and mysterious.

But what is most pleasant about him is his performance in the classroom. His teaching is as magnetic as his appearance. Most students at my school hope he will be their teacher. Without a doubt, he is a popular man.

Name of student _____ Date of testing _____

Grade 7: Form D

Mr. Winters is the most unusual teacher I have ever seen. He is   13
not unattractive, yet he certainly wouldn't be defined as   22
handsome. He is extremely tall and pencil-thin. Looking at him, you   33
feel a jolt of surprise; you definitely have to take a second look.   46

Peculiar is probably the word to describe his looks. A wild   57
shock of mousy brown hair rests on his head like a squirrel's nest   70
abandoned for the winter. His long, pointy face brings to mind   81
images of rocky cliffs, with his nose being the tallest mountain of   93
them all. His glasses, which constantly need to be pushed up, are   105
like a climber desperately trying to scale this peak. Yet, the goal of   118
reaching the zenith consistently slips out of the glasses' grasp.   128
Mr. Winters is always adorned in brown. An occasional glimpse of   139
color may be spotted on a handkerchief that peeks from the   150
pocket of his suit coat.   155

What makes Mr. Winters truly remarkable is his voice. Listeners   165
expect a high, frail voice to match his frame, and so it is a true   180
shock to hear the deep, gravelly boom that escapes his lips. The   192
combination of weak and strong that he embodies makes him   202
intriguing and mysterious.   205

But what is most pleasant about him is his performance in the   217
classroom. His teaching is as magnetic as his appearance. Most   227
students at my school hope he will be their teacher. Without a   239
doubt, he is a popular man.   245

Word Count – 245

Scoring

Word recognition accuracy:

$$\frac{\text{Words correct}}{\text{Total words read orally}} = \underline{\hspace{1cm}} = \underline{\hspace{1cm}} \%$$

Fluency-Automaticity: _____ wcpm

Multidimensional Fluency Scale

Expression and Volume: _____

Phrasing and Intonation: _____

Smoothness: _____

Pace: _____

Total Score: _____

Comprehension: _____

Comments and Observations:

Test Passages

GRADE 8 BOOKLET:

Student Passages and Teacher Pages

As recent immigrants to the United States, my family and I decided to take a trip to see the Statue of Liberty. This symbol of freedom and strength was something we had read about for many years. We wanted to experience it firsthand. Waiting for the ferry to take us to Liberty Island was a wonderful opportunity for "people watching." We were not alone in our interest to see this landmark. All types of people from all corners of the world were crushed together on the dock.

The trip to the island was both exhilarating and fascinating. The smells of sea and city blended together in the wind, which seemed to blow a feeling of history and vitality. The statue herself was an awesome sight to behold. Standing at her feet, I found it difficult to comprehend the masses of people who had stood there before me.

We had hoped to walk up to the statue's crown. However, this was not to be. It was once possible to climb the stairs or take an elevator to the top of the statue. However, recent renovations along with security concerns now prohibit going beyond the statue's base. Instead, my family and I stood outside at the bottom of Lady Liberty, looking up. We marveled at how high the top of the statue appeared from below. We also spent some time on the grounds viewing the magnificent skyline of New York City. It took our breath away.

Visiting this symbol of freedom was an experience I will never forget. It is easy to see why the Statue of Liberty is one of the most important symbols of freedom and democracy in the world.

Name of student _____ Date of testing _____

Grade 8: Form A

As recent immigrants to the United States, my family and I	11
decided to take a trip to see the Statue of Liberty. This symbol of	25
freedom and strength was something we had read about for	35
many years. We wanted to experience it firsthand. Waiting for the	46
ferry to take us to Liberty Island was a wonderful opportunity for	58
"people watching." We were not alone in our interest to see this	70
landmark. All types of people from all corners of the world were	82
crushed together on the dock.	87
The trip to the island was both exhilarating and fascinating.	97
The smells of sea and city blended together in the wind, which	109
seemed to blow a feeling of history and vitality. The statue herself	121
was an awesome sight to behold. Standing at her feet, I found it	134
difficult to comprehend the masses of people who had stood	144
there before me.	147
We had hoped to walk up to the statue's crown. However, this	159
was not to be. It was once possible to climb the stairs or take an	174
elevator to the top of the statue. However, recent renovations	184
along with security concerns now prohibit going beyond the	193
statue's base. Instead, my family and I stood outside at the	204
bottom of Lady Liberty, looking up. We marveled at how high the	216
top of the statue appeared from below. We also spent some time	228
on the grounds viewing the magnificent skyline of New York City. It	240
took our breath away.	244
Visiting this symbol of freedom was an experience I will never	255
forget. It is easy to see why the Statue of Liberty is one of the most	271
important symbols of freedom and democracy in the world.	280

Word Count – 280

Scoring

Word recognition accuracy:

Words correct
———————————— = _____ = _____ %
Total words read orally

Fluency-Automaticity: _____ wcpm

Multidimensional Fluency Scale

Expression and Volume: _____

Phrasing and Intonation: _____

Smoothness: ____ ____

Pace: _____

Total Score: _____

Comprehension: _____

Comments and Observations:

Here's a word that comes to mind when I think of Brussels sprouts: *repulsive*. They are truly among the foulest foods ever invented. My mother prepares them whenever my grandparents come for dinner. I have reached the point where just sitting at the table with Grandma and Grandpa sends shivers down my spine. It makes me wish for the days of the children's table where unpopular foods ended up in the trash can or the dog's mouth. Brussels sprouts were created to punish children for everything they have ever done wrong. I think some parents look forward to the day when they can exact revenge upon their children for all the years when they had to eat Brussels sprouts themselves.

Although my mother and father say they are an excellent source of vitamins and minerals, I know they are capsules of horror wrapped in deceptively adorable little packages. Sitting in the bowl on the dining room table they may look harmless, even decorative. But once on your plate, their appearance changes dramatically. You are faced with an enemy that refuses to be swallowed whole. These so-called sprouts strive to leave a metallic aftertaste in your mouth, reminding you of their victory.

Do not be fooled by those who claim that your health is the reason that this vegetable is being served. Tell your parents that you are sick and retire to your room. An empty stomach is much better than the alternative: a plate full of Brussels sprouts.

Name of student _____ Date of testing _____

Grade 8: Form B

Here's a word that comes to mind when I think of Brussels	12
sprouts: *repulsive*. They are truly among the foulest foods ever	22
invented. My mother prepares them whenever my grandparents	30
come for dinner. I have reached the point where just sitting at the	43
table with Grandma and Grandpa sends shivers down my spine. It	54
makes me wish for the days of the children's table where	65
unpopular foods ended up in the trash can or the dog's mouth.	77
Brussels sprouts were created to punish children for everything	86
they have ever done wrong. I think some parents look forward to	98
the day when they can exact revenge upon their children for all	110
the years when they had to eat Brussels sprouts themselves.	120

Although my mother and father say they are an excellent	130
source of vitamins and minerals, I know they are capsules of horror	142
wrapped in deceptively adorable little packages. Sitting in the	151
bowl on the dining room table they may look harmless, even	162
decorative. But once on your plate, their appearance changes	171
dramatically. You are faced with an enemy that refuses to be	182
swallowed whole. These so-called sprouts strive to leave a metallic	192
aftertaste in your mouth, reminding you of their victory.	201

Do not be fooled by those who claim that your health is the	214
reason that this vegetable is being served. Tell your parents that	225
you are sick and retire to your room. An empty stomach is much	238
better than the alternative: a plate full of Brussels sprouts.	248

Word Count – 248

Scoring

Word recognition accuracy:

$$\frac{\text{Words correct}}{\text{Total words read orally}} = \text{_____} = \text{_____} \%$$

Fluency-Automaticity: _____ wcpm

Multidimensional Fluency Scale

Expression and Volume: _____

Phrasing and Intonation: _____

Smoothness: _____

Pace: _____

Total Score: _____

Comprehension: _____

Comments and Observations:

The intense heat sears my back as I slowly cross the parking lot to enter the shopping mall. The black pavement, a sea of molten tar, seems to boil beneath my sneakers. It licks the soles of my shoes, trying to melt them with its dark, fiery breath. The air has turned hazy, and everywhere I look it seems blurred and watery. The sun, a bright circle, appears to be floating just inches from the top of my head. Its heat emanates in pulses, pushing through the thick atmosphere like waves pounding against my body.

Broadcast from every surrounding car are voices predicting the day's record high temperatures. These reporters, no doubt sitting in air-conditioned comfort, warn me to drink plenty of water, stay indoors, and take care of the elderly and my pets.

Each step is an effort. I am in conflict as to whether I should hurry up and get to my destination or stop right where I am. The double doors to the mall are within sight. They are calling to me, offering solace from this nightmare I am living. I use all my will and determination and force my legs to carry me through the last stretch of heated wind that is pushing me back. Finally, I enter through the doors of the mall and am greeted with a blast of frigid air that meets me like my family after years of separation. I know what awaits me outside, but for now I am encompassed within a cocoon of comfort and safety.

Grade 8: Form C

The intense heat sears my back as I slowly cross the parking lot	13
to enter the shopping mall. The black pavement, a sea of molten	25
tar, seems to boil beneath my sneakers. It licks the soles of my	38
shoes, trying to melt them with its dark, fiery breath. The air has	51
turned hazy, and everywhere I look it seems blurred and watery.	62
The sun, a bright circle, appears to be floating just inches from the	75
top of my head. Its heat emanates in pulses, pushing through the	87
thick atmosphere like waves pounding against my body.	95
Broadcast from every surrounding car are voices predicting	103
the day's record high temperatures. These reporters, no doubt	112
sitting in air-conditioned comfort, warn me to drink plenty of	122
water, stay indoors, and take care of the elderly and my pets.	134
Each step is an effort. I am in conflict as to whether I should	148
hurry up and get to my destination or stop right where I am. The	162
double doors to the mall are within sight. They are calling to me,	175
offering solace from this nightmare I am living. I use all my will and	189
determination and force my legs to carry me through the last	200
stretch of heated wind that is pushing me back. Finally, I enter	212
through the doors of the mall and am greeted with a blast of frigid	226
air that meets me like my family after years of separation. I know	239
what awaits me outside, but for now I am encompassed within a	251
cocoon of comfort and safety.	256

Word Count – 256

Scoring

Word recognition accuracy:

$$\frac{\text{Words correct}}{\text{Total words read orally}} = \text{_____} = \text{_____} \%$$

Fluency-Automaticity: _____ wcpm

Multidimensional Fluency Scale

Expression and Volume: _____

Phrasing and Intonation: _____

Smoothness: _____

Pace: _____

Total Score: _____

Comprehension: _____

Comments and Observations:

TEACHER PAGE ■

FORM C

GRADE 8

A tiny bundle of joy is what my father called her. That's not altogether accurate from my perspective. It was my sister Jane who helped me understand the phrase, "wailing like a banshee." From the wee hours of the night through the day and back again, Jane's vocal cords were in constant use. Although this intense and constant screaming lasted only a few months, I still feel the ramifications of her arrival to this day. This little bundle of joy is now three years old and is a perpetual interference in my daily life.

Jane's baby cries have turned into a preschooler's incessant chatter. Every morning I awake to two blue eyes staring into mine. I stagger out of bed to the bathroom while barrages of meaningless questions are fired at me, seemingly without interest in my response. Throughout breakfast I work diligently to steer Jane's attentions toward my parents so I might stealthily slip out unnoticed and make my way to school. It seems as if school is the only safe haven from my energetic young sister.

Upon my return from school each day I am greeted anew by that bundle of energy. Refreshed from her afternoon nap, Jane is ready for frolic and fun. Occasionally, for the sole purpose of appeasing her long enough to earn the right to escape, I agree to play with her (but only for a moment or two). An ugly dinosaur is handed to me, and I am ordered to make scary dinosaur noises. With every noise I make, she reciprocates with a high-pitched scream from her baby doll's mouth. Annoyed at first, I can't help noticing how cute Jane really is, and how maybe playing with dinosaurs and dolls isn't that bad after all. I'll never admit it out loud, but I kind of like having a little sister around.

Name of student _____ Date of testing _____

Grade 8: Form D

A tiny bundle of joy is what my father called her. That's not	13
altogether accurate from my perspective. It was my sister Jane	23
who helped me understand the phrase, "wailing like a banshee."	33
From the wee hours of the night through the day and back again,	46
Jane's vocal cords were in constant use. Although this intense and	57
constant screaming lasted only a few months, I still feel the	68
ramifications of her arrival to this day. This little bundle of joy is now	82
three years old and is a perpetual interference in my daily life.	94

Jane's baby cries have turned into a preschooler's incessant	103
chatter. Every morning I awake to two blue eyes staring into mine.	115
I stagger out of bed to the bathroom while barrages of	126
meaningless questions are fired at me, seemingly without interest	135
in my response. Throughout breakfast I work diligently to steer	145
Jane's attentions toward my parents so I might stealthily slip out	156
unnoticed and make my way to school. It seems as if school is the	170
only safe haven from my energetic young sister.	178

Upon my return from school each day I am greeted anew by	190
that bundle of energy. Refreshed from her afternoon nap, Jane is	201
ready for frolic and fun. Occasionally, for the sole purpose of	212
appeasing her long enough to earn the right to escape, I agree to	225
play with her (but only for a moment or two). An ugly dinosaur is	239
handed to me, and I am ordered to make scary dinosaur noises.	251
With every noise I make, she reciprocates with a high-pitched	261
scream from her baby doll's mouth. Annoyed at first, I can't help	273
noticing how cute Jane really is, and how maybe playing with	284
dinosaurs and dolls isn't that bad after all. I'll never admit it out	297
loud, but I kind of like having a little sister around.	308

Word Count – 308

Scoring

Word recognition accuracy:

$$\frac{\text{Words correct}}{\text{Total words read orally}} = \underline{\hspace{2cm}} = \underline{\hspace{1.5cm}} \%$$

Fluency-Automaticity: _____ wcpm

Multidimensional Fluency Scale

Expression and Volume: _____

Phrasing and Intonation: _____

Smoothness: _____

Pace: _____

Total Score: _____

Comprehension: _____

Comments and Observations:

CLASS RECORD SHEET

Student Name	Date of Testing	Word Recognition Accuracy	Fluency-Automaticity (wcpm)	Multidimensional Fluency Scale	Expression and Volume	Phrasing and Intonation	Smoothness	Pace	Comprehension	Date of Testing	Word Recognition Accuracy	Fluency-Automaticity (wcpm)	Multidimensional Fluency Scale	Expression and Volume	Phrasing and Intonation	Smoothness	Pace	Comprehension	Date of Testing	Word Recognition Accuracy	Fluency-Automaticity (wcpm)	Multidimensional Fluency Scale	Expression and Volume	Phrasing and Intonation	Smoothness	Pace	Comprehension	Date of Testing	Word Recognition Accuracy	Fluency-Automaticity (wcpm)	Multidimensional Fluency Scale	Expression and Volume	Phrasing and Intonation	Smoothness	Pace	Comprehension

INDIVIDUAL STUDENT RECORD SHEET

Teacher: _____

Student: _____

Grade: _____

School Year: _____

	Score	Comments
Form A Date of Administration: _____		
Word Recognition Accuracy		
Fluency-Automaticity (wcpm)		
Multidimensional Fluency Scale		
Expression and Volume		
Phrasing and Intonation		
Smoothness		
Pace		
Comprehension		
Form B Date of Administration: _____		
Word Recognition Accuracy		
Fluency-Automaticity (wcpm)		
Multidimensional Fluency Scale		
Expression and Volume		
Phrasing and Intonation		
Smoothness		
Pace		
Comprehension		
Form C Date of Administration: _____		
Word Recognition Accuracy		
Fluency-Automaticity (wcpm)		
Multidimensional Fluency Scale		
Expression and Volume		
Phrasing and Intonation		
Smoothness		
Pace		
Comprehension		
Form D Date of Administration: _____		
Word Recognition Accuracy		
Fluency-Automaticity (wcpm)		
Multidimensional Fluency Scale		
Expression and Volume		
Phrasing and Intonation		
Smoothness		
Pace		
Comprehension		

Instructional Ideas for Word Recognition, Fluency, and Comprehension

Word Recognition Instruction

For students experiencing difficulty in word recognition (percentage accuracy 90% or less while reading a grade-level passage), consider the following instructional ideas:

◆ Teach high-frequency words—for example, the Dolch List and the Fry Instant Word List. Teach five words a week, and practice them daily. Put the words on the word wall, and review the word wall each day. Play games with the words. Have students write the words while saying and spelling them.

◆ Teach common word families (phonograms or rimes—for example, *-at* in *cat* and *bat*). List and practice words belonging to the word family. Read poetry and other texts that contain the targeted word families. Have students write their own poems using words belonging to a word family. Add words studied from the word families to the classroom word wall.

◆ Have students sort words from the word wall or from some other source of words by various categories—by a particular vowel or consonant sound, by grammatical category, by some meaningful attribute of the word, and so on.

◆ Use flash cards and other practice activities for words under study. Keep these activities game-like and brief—no more than 5–10 minutes—and conduct them once or twice per day.

◆ Engage in word-building activities such as Making Words or Making and Writing Words. Provide students with a limited set of letters and guide them through the process of building (writing) words using those letters. Draw students' attention to the meaning, sound, and spelling of the words.

◆ Teach students to decode multisyllabic words. Teach basic syllabication rules (for example, in words with two vowels that are separated by one consonant, the word is normally divided into syllables after the first vowel [*hotel, pilot, final*]; syllables that end in a vowel usually have the long vowel sound [*secret, baby, pilot*]).

◆ Help students detect prefixes, suffixes, and base words in longer words (for example, *replay, cowboy, basement*). Teach students how breaking larger words into prefixes, suffixes, and base words can help them to decode the larger word and determine its meaning.

◆ Use the cloze procedure to teach contextual word recognition. Find an appropriate text and delete words that can be determined from the context. Have students read the text with the deleted words and determine the missing words using the contextual information in the passage.

◆ Engage students in occasional conversations about *how* they decode unfamiliar words. During this work on self-monitoring, focus on confirmation as well by asking questions such as "How did you know you were right?"

◈ Encourage students to read at home and to practice words at home as well as in school.

◈ Engage students in games and game-like activities, such as word-based Wheel of Fortune, Go Fish, Concentration, and Wordo (word bingo) that give them the opportunity to practice the words they are studying.

◈ Use the fluency-building activities listed on the following pages to build word recognition skills as well as overall reading fluency.

◈ Provide students with plenty of opportunities to read texts that contain words they are studying.

◈ Develop a daily instructional routine (20–30 minutes) devoted to the various activities described in this section. Use some of the activities in this section in a systematic and regular way with students who are experiencing difficulty in learning to decode words.

Fluency Instruction

For students experiencing difficulty in reading fluency (reading rate less than the accepted norms while reading a grade-level passage), consider the following instructional ideas:

◈ Read to students on a regular basis. As you do so, be sure to model for them what fluent reading is like. Ask them to listen for the way you use your voice to convey meaning. If the students have a copy of the text you are reading, have them follow along silently while you read to them.

◈ Have individual students read a passage aloud while listening to you or another reader read with them. This is known as "assisted [paired] reading." The combination of a student's reading a text while listening to someone else read it fluently is a well-known means of improving fluency and comprehension. Make this a daily 10–15 minute routine. If no one is available to read with the student, record the reading on tape and have the student read the passage while listening to it on tape.

◈ Develop a daily home routine in which a parent sits side by side with the child and engages in assisted reading with the child for 10–15 minutes. If parents are not available, students may read while listening to a recorded version of the passage.

◈ Have students practice reading a passage (100–250 words in length) several times until they are able to read it accurately, quickly, and expressively. This technique, known as "repeated [practice] reading," may require 7 or 8 readings. The practice may occur over a period of several days and may be done at home as well as in school. Make this a daily classroom activity; once students have mastered one passage, have them move on to other equally or more challenging passages. Passages that are meant to be performed (for example, poetry, scripts, speeches) work very well to promote practiced and expressive reading.

◆ Combine repeated and assisted reading. Have students practice reading a passage several times until they are able to read it fluently. In addition to practicing the passage independently, students may also practice the passage while listening to a partner read it with them or while listening to a recorded version of the passage.

◆ Develop integrated fluency instructional routines—daily routines for fostering fluency that combine modeling, assisted reading, and repeated readings. The Fluency Development Lesson, described below, is one example of an integrated fluency routine.

- Work with a daily passage of 100–250 words that lends itself to expressive and interpretive reading. Make two copies of the passage for every student in the group.

- Read the passage to students several times while they follow along. Discuss the passage with students.

- Read the passage chorally several times with students.

- Next, have students work in pairs. Ideally, each pair should have its own quiet place in which to work. Have one student read the passage two or three times while the partner follows along silently and provides assistance when necessary. When the first reader has finished, the partners switch roles and repeat the process.

- Have student pairs perform their passage for their classmates or other audiences.

- Select interesting words from the passage and add them to the word wall for further practice, sorting, and use in writing.

- Place one copy of the passage into students' fluency folders for future practice. Send the other copy home for additional practice with parents.

- The following morning, begin by having students read the passage from the previous day. Then, begin a new lesson with a new passage.

◆ Provide students with daily time (15–20 minutes) for independent reading. Ensure that students read material that is at their independent reading level. Make students accountable for their independent reading time by having them summarize their daily reading in a reading journal. Alternately, you might have students read aloud (in a soft voice) during the independent reading period so that you can be assured they are actually reading the text.

Comprehension Instruction

For students experiencing difficulty in comprehension (retelling rated in the lower range on the comprehension rubric while reading a grade-level passage), consider the following instructional ideas:

◆ Before asking students to read a passage, ensure that they have sufficient background knowledge. You may increase background knowledge in a variety of ways:

- Provide information to students by telling them directly.

- Brainstorm background information with students.

- Read related material to students that will increase background knowledge.

- Use other print and non-print media such as movies, videotapes, the Internet, artifacts (for example, maps, music, food) to expand background knowledge.

- Bring in others who are knowledgeable about a topic to share information and personal experience with students.

◆ Use text maps or graphics with students. Present students with a text map or graphic that demonstrates the organization of the main ideas in a passage. This can be done before reading a passage. Alternately, give students a partially completed map or graphic to complete while they are reading a passage. Or provide an empty graphic for students and ask them to use it to make notes while they read.

◆ Once students are familiar with the idea of text maps and graphics, ask them to develop their own maps or graphics after reading a passage. The map or graphic should reflect the meaning of the passage and the overall organization of the ideas in the text.

◆ After reading a passage together, engage students in a lively discussion about it. Make sure the discussion goes beyond recitation of information contained in the passage. Encourage students to make reasoned inferences about the passage. Ask them to share opinions and ideas, always reminding them to provide justification for their assertions.

◆ Engage students in making predictions or hypotheses about what will happen next as they read. Ask them to justify their predictions and use the predictions as the basis for discussion of the passage with others.

◆ Ask students to develop relevant questions related to the passage before, during, and after reading it. Use these questions to guide discussion of the material.

◆ Select texts that lend themselves to image creation and encourage students to create images while they read these texts. Images can be internal mental images or actual drawings students make during and after reading. Have students use the images as a starting point for discussing the passage with others.

◆ Instruct students to take written notes (along with insights, observations, wonderings, and questions) while reading a passage, trying to capture in their notes the important ideas that are presented in the text. After reading and taking notes, students should use the notes to write a summary of the passage. Tell students to refer to their notes when discussing the passage.

◆ Encourage students to react to their reading by writing in journals or learning logs. Entries can be general reactions or focused responses (for example, favorite character, most important idea, most interesting part). For expository text, ask students to make log entries describing new processes or providing definitions of important concepts.

◆ Allow students to respond to a reading (re-represent the main ideas of a passage) in creative ways. These include:

  ● creating tableaux (performances of a passage in which students assume different stances, keeping their bodies motionless, to portray the essential meaning),

  ● finding or developing a poem or song in response to the reading,

  ● creating an advertisement that represents the main idea of a passage,

  ● writing a journal entry or letter from the point of view of one of the characters in the passage,

  ● choosing and explaining a metaphor that reflects a character or event from a passage, or

  ● developing a diorama that captures the essence of a text.

◆ Instruct students on how to read and use information that is presented pictorially or graphically—in charts, tables, figures, maps, and graphs.

References

Beaver, J. (1997). *Developmental reading assessment.* Upper Saddle River, NJ: Pearson.

Biemiller, A. (2003). Oral comprehension sets the ceiling on reading comprehension. *American Educator, 23,* 44.

Clay, M. M. (1993). *Reading Recovery: A guidebook for teachers in training.* Portsmouth, NH: Heinemann.

Leslie, L., & Caldwell, J. (2000). *Qualitative reading inventory* (3rd ed.). Upper Saddle River, NJ: Pearson.

Postlethwaite, T. N., & Ross, K. N. (1992). *Effective schools in reading: Implications for educational planners.* The Hague: International Association for the Evaluation of Educational Achievement.

Stanford diagnostic reading test. San Antonio, TX: Harcourt.

Woodcock reading mastery test. Circle Pines, MN: American Guidance Service.

Zutell, J. & Rasinski, T. V. (1991). Training teachers to attend to their students' oral reading fluency. *Theory into Practice, 30,* 211-217.

Notes

Notes

3-Minute Reading Assessments: Word Recognition, Fluency, and Comprehension—Grades 5–8 Scholastic Teaching Resources